Excel® for Microsoft 365® Introduction

Need to know general things that apply to all Microsoft products like opening and saving files, or how to undo a mistake? See our **Microsoft 365 Essentials** guide.

Entering New Data

1. [Click] on a cell, or move to it with the arrow keys.
2. Type the data. If you make a mistake while typing, press <Backspace> to delete characters.
3. Press <Enter> or [Click] ✓ in the Formula Bar.

The Formula Bar is located between your worksheet and the Ribbon, and displays the data or formula stored in the active cell.

If Excel suggests an entry, press <Enter> to accept, <Delete> to remove, or ignore it by continuing to type.

Picking from a Drop-Down List

To pick from a list of text values already entered in cells below or above the active cell, press <Alt-↓>, then use arrows and <Enter> to select. Or, [Right Click] the cell, then choose PICK FROM DROP-DOWN LIST.

Editing the Contents of a Cell

1. [Click] on the cell to change.
2. [Click] in the Formula Bar. Or, to edit directly in the cell, [Double Click] the cell or press <F2>.
3. Use arrow keys to move, <Backspace> to delete left, <Delete> to delete right, or type text to insert.
4. When finished, press <Enter> or [Click] ✓.

To cancel editing: [Click] ✗ or press <Esc>.

Replacing the Contents of a Cell

1. [Click] on or move to the cell to change.
2. Type new data, then press <Enter> or [Click] ✓.

Selecting Cells

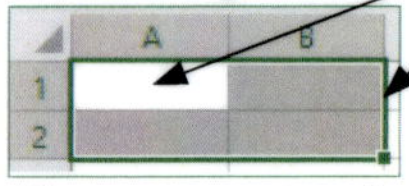

Active cell is white.
Selected cells are surrounded by a solid border.

When you type, the value is inserted in the active cell.

To select a single cell: [Click] the cell, or use the arrow keys to move to the cell.

To select a range of cells: [Drag] across cells, or:

- <Shift>-[Click] a cell other than the active cell.
- Hold <Shift> while using the arrow keys.
- Tap, Drag.

To select entire rows/columns: [Click] headings A B or 1 2

To select entire worksheet: [Click] where the row and column headings meet.

To select multiple ranges: Select a range, press <Ctrl> while selecting more ranges.

Resizing Column Width or Row Height

To change several columns/rows at once, select them first.

1. [Point] at the dividing line between the column or row headings. The mouse pointer changes into a double-headed arrow ✛ or ✛.
2. [Drag] to change the width or height. Or, to AutoFit to the widest/highest cell, [Double Click] the line.

Or to enter a measurement:

1. Select a cell in the row/column to adjust.
2. Choose HOME, FORMAT, either ROW HEIGHT or COLUMN WIDTH.
3. Enter a height or width, then [Click] OK.

Inserting Rows or Columns

1. Select a row or column heading. New columns insert to the left, and rows above the selection. To insert several rows or columns, select that number of rows or columns.
2. Choose HOME, then INSERT.

Inserting Cells

1. Select the cells where you wish to insert new ones.
2. Choose HOME, Insert, then INSERT CELLS.
3. Specify direction to shift the selected cells. [Click] OK.

Clearing Cells

You can clear the contents of cells, cell formatting, or both content and formatting.

1. Select the cells to clear.
2. To clear contents only (not formatting): Choose HOME, Clear, CLEAR CONTENTS. Or, press <Delete>.
   To clear only formatting: Choose CLEAR FORMATS.
   To clear everything: Choose CLEAR ALL.

Deleting Rows, Columns, or Cells

As compared to clearing (described above) this removes the cells and moves surrounding cells to fill the gap.

To delete rows or columns:

1. Select the row(s) or column(s), using headings.
2. Choose HOME, then DELETE.

To delete cells:

1. Select the cell(s).
2. Choose HOME, Delete, then DELETE CELLS.
3. Specify direction to shift surrounding cells. [Click] OK.

Borders, Shading, Text Color

Select cells, then choose HOME, and [Click] one of: (Borders, Fill Color, Font Color).

Drawing a Border Grid

1. Choose HOME, then [Click] drop-down arrow of (Borders), then select DRAW BORDER or, to draw a grid, select DRAW BORDER GRID.
2. [Drag] to create one or more borders, then [Click] (Draw Border) or press <Esc>.

Erasing a Border

1. Choose HOME, then [Click] drop-down arrow of (Borders), then select ERASE BORDER.
2. [Drag] across or [Click] the borders to erase.
3. [Click] (Erase Border) or press <Esc>.

Formatting Number Cells

A cell's format affects the way its value is displayed, but it doesn't change the underlying value, or the way it is filtered, sorted, or calculated.

1. Select the cells to format. This can be done before or after the data has been entered.
2. Choose HOME, then a format from the Number Format list General, found in the NUMBER group.
   Or, [Click] one of the following buttons:

$	Formats as default currency with 2 decimals. [Click] drop-down arrow for other currencies.
%	Formats as a percentage.
,	Displays commas between thousands, and two decimal places.
←.0 .00	Adds a decimal place with each [Click].
.00 →.0	Removes a decimal place with each [Click].

Aligning and Merging Cells

To align within the cell, select the cells to align, then choose HOME, then one of (vertical alignment buttons) or (horizontal alignment buttons).

To merge cells and center the contents, select the cells to merge across, and [Click] Merge & Center.

Other merge options, including UNMERGE CELLS, are available in the drop-down list.

Entering Dates

For dates to be used in formulas, enter them using one of Excel's date formats, e.g., 3/14/19 or 14-Mar-19.

To change how dates display for specific cells:

1. Select the cells containing dates.
2. Choose HOME, then MORE NUMBER FORMATS from the Number Format list General.
3. From the DATE category, select a TYPE. "*" indicates it is affected by the date format set in Windows [Click] OK.

Entering a Sequence of Numbers

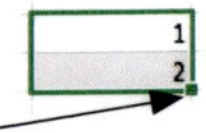

1. Enter the first two numbers or dates of the sequence into adjacent cells.
2. Select the two cells.
3. [Drag] the Fill handl… cells.

For mor…

1. Enter…
2. Select… with t…
3. Choos…
4. Specify… …xample, to fill only with weekdays: in TYPE, choose DATE, then WEEKDAY. [Click] OK.

Touch Actions

Click/Double Click	Tap/Double Tap
Scroll	Drag or Swipe
Select text	Tap, Drag
Zoom in/out	Stretch/Pinch
Right Click menu	Touch and hold for box
Touch Mini Toolbar	Tap text/picture/etc. then tap again. Or, touch and hold for box. Tap drop-down arrow to see more options.

To improve your touch experience, turn on the touch-optimized Ribbon and status bar (some buttons change to menus): in Quick Access Toolbar (Touch/Mouse Mode), then TOUCH.

Moving Within the Worksheet

One cell up or down	↑ or ↓
Cell to the right	→ or Tab
Cell to the left	← or Shift-Tab
Within selected cells	Tab, Enter, Shift-Tab, Shift-Enter
Beginning of the row	Home
Cell A1	Ctrl-Home
Intersection of the last used row and column	Ctrl-End
One screenful down/up	Page down/up
One screenful right/left	Alt-Page down/up
To the last filled cell in any direction, or if in a blank cell, to the next filled cell	Ctrl-Arrow Key
To a cell that you specify	F5, type cell, OK or Shift-OK to select to the new cell
Next or previous sheet	Ctrl-PgDn or Ctrl-PgUp

<Shift> with any of these movement shortcuts will select from the current cell to that location. E.g., <Shift-Ctrl-Home> selects from the current cell back to cell A1.

Selection Shortcuts

An entire row	Shift-Spacebar
An entire column	Ctrl-Spacebar
The entire worksheet	Ctrl-Shift-Spacebar, repeat if needed.

Formulas

Create a formula in a cell to manipulate or calculate data. The formula can contain references to data in other cells as well as numbers, arithmetic operators, and functions. The basic arithmetic operators used in formulas are:

+ addition * multiplication
- subtraction / division

All formulas begin with an equals sign (=).

B3 =B1-B2

	A	B	C
1	Revenue	1850	
2	Expenses	1320	
3	Profit	530	

The formula in cell B3 subtracts the value in cell B2 from cell B1.

The Formula Bar displays the formula =B1-B2 when the formula cell is active, and the worksheet cell displays the result. Use ( ) parentheses to surround parts of a formula to be calculated first, e.g., =(B2+B5+B8)*.02

Entering a Formula

1. [Click] the cell in which the result is to appear.
2. Type =, then the rest of the formula. Instead of typing a cell reference you can also [Click] on the cell, or select a range of cells.
3. Press <Enter>, or [Click] ✓.

Some examples:
=B2*C2
=B8*50%
=(C4+C9)/C10

Functions

A function is a pre-built complex formula that you refer to by name. It greatly simplifies the creation of a formula and can be combined with other calculations into a larger formula.

Some commonly used functions:

=SUM(B1:B50) Adds the numbers in the range.

=AVERAGE(B1:B50) Averages numbers in a range. Blank cells are ignored; zeroes are averaged.

=MAX(B1:B50) Returns the highest number in the range. (MIN returns lowest)

=TODAY( ) Enters the current date.

When typing in a function, a ScreenTip shows what needs to be specified for that function:

=round(
ROUND(**number**, num_digits)

For detailed help, use the Insert Function button:

1. [Click] a cell, or place the cursor within a formula where the function is to be inserted. [Click] fx.
2. SELECT A FUNCTION or SELECT A CATEGORY first. [Click] OK.
3. Each input needed by the function is displayed as a field with a description below when selected. Mandatory fields are bold. Specify cell references, ranges, numbers, or text values in the fields. To temporarily compress the dialog box [Click] , make a selection, [Click] . [Click] OK.

Functions can be part of a larger formula, e.g., **=SUM(B1:B50)/C2 or =SUM(B1:B50)/SUM(C1:C50)**

Quick Entry of SUM & Other Functions

1. [Click] the cell in which the result is to appear.
2. Choose HOME, then Σ AutoSum.

   To insert Average, Count, Max, or Min instead of Sum, [Click] the drop-down arrow.
3. Adjust the range if needed, then [Click] ✓ or press <Enter>.

Absolute vs. Relative Cell References

- Relative: A relative reference (e.g., A5) changes when copied, maintaining the relative position of the referenced cell(s) to the formula cell. For example, it always references the cell "two to the left."
- Absolute: An absolute reference (e.g., A5) stays exactly the same when copied.

For example, the rate in B1 (absolute reference) will be multiplied by the value "one cell to the left" (relative reference) when the formula is copied down the column:

	A	B
1	Rate	1.06
2		
3	504	=B1*A3
4	360	381.6
5	6930	7345.8

Note: While typing a cell reference, you can quickly make it absolute by pressing <F4>.

Moving and Copying Cells

Copying to Adjacent Cells

1. Select the cell to copy.
2. [Point] at the Fill handle in the bottom right corner. The mouse pointer will change to a thin plus sign.
3. [Drag] into the empty cells. Some data produces a sequence, e.g., January, Monday, Quarter 1. If this is not wanted, hold down <Ctrl> to force a copy.

Cut, Copy, Paste

1. Select the cell(s).
2. To move, choose HOME, then , or press <Ctrl-X>.

   To copy, choose HOME, then , or press <Ctrl-C>.
3. [Click] on the top left cell of the new location.
4. [Click] PASTE , or press <Ctrl-V>.

   For paste options, or to preview the paste, [Click] Paste and [Hover] over the options.

   Or, after pasting, press <Ctrl> or [Click] (Ctrl) PASTE OPTIONS next to the pasted data.

Drag and Drop

1. Select the cells to move or copy.
2. [Point] at the outline around the selected cells (avoiding the Fill handle). The mouse pointer will change .
3. To move cells, [Drag] the selection to the new location. To move to a new sheet, press <Alt> while you [Drag] over a worksheet tab.

   To copy cells, press <Ctrl> while you [Drag].

   To move and insert, press <Shift> while you [Drag]. A horizontal bar indicates insert and shift cells down, a vertical bar indicates insert and shift cells right.

   <Ctrl>, <Alt>, and <Shift> can be combined.

Inserting a Sheet

- [Click] ⊕ below the worksheet.
- Choose HOME, then Insert then INSERT SHEET.

Renaming a Sheet

[Double Click] the sheet tab, e.g., Sheet1, then type the new name and press <Enter>.

Moving Among Sheets

- [Click] on the sheet tab. If the sheet tab is not visible, [Click] ◂ or ▸.
- To show the first/last tab press <Ctrl> then [Click] ◂ or ▸.
- To select from a list of all sheet names, [Right Click] ◂ or ▸.

Moving or Copying Sheets

To move, [Drag] the sheet tab to the new position, even to another workbook if visible. To copy, press <Ctrl> while you [Drag].

Deleting a Sheet

- [Right Click] the sheet tab, then choose DELETE.
- Choose HOME, Delete, then DELETE SHEET.

Selecting Sheets

- Adjacent sheets: [Click] on the sheet tab at one end, and <Shift>-[Click] on the tab at the other end.
- Non-adjacent sheets: <Ctrl>-[Click] on sheet tabs.
- All sheets: [Right Click] a sheet tab and choose SELECT ALL SHEETS.
- To deselect one sheet: <Ctrl>-[Click] the sheet (it cannot be the active sheet). To deselect all: [Click] on a sheet tab that is not selected. If all are selected, [Click] on any sheet tab except the active one.

Editing Sheets Simultaneously

When multiple sheets are selected, they become grouped. Any changes you make to one sheet, will also change all other selected sheets. The title bar of the workbook will show **- Group -** while in this mode. When finished, be sure to exit group mode by deselecting sheets (see above).

Viewing the Worksheet as it Will Print

To show the worksheet as it will print while you work, [Click] in the status bar at the bottom.

Printing the Worksheet

1. Choose FILE, PRINT.
2. Review the preview, optionally change PRINTER or SETTINGS. To show drag-able margins, [Click] in bottom right.
3. [Click] PRINT .

Fitting Printout to Pages

To constrain the worksheet to a certain number of pages, choose PAGE LAYOUT, then page limits from Width: and Height: .

Printing a Specific Area

To set a print area that is saved with the file:

1. Select the range to print.
2. Choose PAGE LAYOUT, then PRINT AREA , then SET PRINT AREA.

   Or, to set another print area for the same worksheet, choose ADD TO PRINT AREA.

To clear the print areas on a worksheet:

Choose PAGE LAYOUT, PRINT AREA , then CLEAR PRINT AREA.

To print a selected area (overrides saved print area):

1. Select the range to print, then choose FILE, PRINT.
2. Set the first drop-down list under SETTINGS to PRINT SELECTION.
3. [Click] PRINT .

Adjusting Page Breaks

1. [Click] in the status bar at the bottom to go to Page Break Preview.
2. [Drag] page breaks to the best position.
3. [Click] when done to return to Normal view.

Repeating Rows/Columns on Every Page

To print headings of a list on every page:

1. Choose PAGE LAYOUT, then PRINT TITLES .
2. [Click] beside ROWS TO REPEAT AT TOP or COLUMNS TO REPEAT AT LEFT, and select the rows and/or columns in the worksheet.
3. [Click] , then OK.

Need to know more? See our other guides.

Beezix Quick Reference Guides
info@beezix.com
beezix.com

ISBN 978-1-944684-78-5